The Six Keys to Confident Change Management

**CHANGE
MANAGEMENT**

The Six Keys to Confident Change Management

By Robert L. Bogue

Editor: Dana Lheureau

While every precaution has been taken in the preparation of this book, the publisher and author assume no responsibility for errors or omissions, or for damages resulting from the use of the information contained herein.

ISBN-10: 0-9824198-4-8

ISBN-13: 978-0-9824198-4-7

Printed in the United States of America

Table of Contents

Introduction

I can remember as a teenager being fundamentally confused. I'd walk down the high school halls and people would be so excited about the latest trends. Jordache jeans, Nike shoes, Swatch watches, Ray Ban glasses and the like were what the cool kids wore, and everyone knew it. Everyone knew it except for me. I never understood why people weren't more practical. Those brand names didn't really do anything better than any other brand – or did they? Were they worth their exorbitant prices or were they just wasting money?

I became intrigued by what made some brands hot and other brands not. I became curious as to why fads came and went while others stayed. However, my curiosity was lost to hazy memories of my adolescence until I ran into the same questions in business.

I have always been practical. I've always wanted to get things done. I spent part of my childhood in the country building things, breaking them, and putting them back together. I learned to be practical. If it worked, then it was good enough. However, at the same time I was aware that farmers had just ended a fifty-year run of impressive improvements in production by trying new things. They were practical by being innovative.

I built solutions, new solutions, with new technology and new ideas. I expected great gains. I expected that the organization would leverage the new technologies that I deployed to better themselves and crush their competition. However, I was surprised when nothing changed. Sure, they could communicate better, more efficiently, and more clearly than ever before, but things stayed the same.

It's a hard lesson to learn that a hammer doesn't make a house. It's in one sense obvious. In another sense, you know that a house can't be made without a hammer, so therefore a hammer should make a house – but it doesn't. I reasoned that the problem with giving organizations hammers was they just didn't know how to use those hammers.

My naivete continued for a while as I created education for the user of the hammers I was deploying to the organization. It was helpful to be sure. They were unfamiliar with the technology, and having guides that would teach them formed an essential bridge to allow them to use the hammer. What I didn't realize is that they didn't want to use a hammer.

I missed Ted Levitt's admonishment, "People don't want to buy a quarter-inch drill, they want a quarter-inch hole." I was still selling the solution instead of solving the real problem. The real problem wasn't that they didn't know how to do something. The real problem was that they didn't know why they wanted to change. So, I started the journey of learning why people want to do things. I started thinking about those 1980s brand names and wondering why people felt like they were worth buying. It seems like they were making a change in their fashion identity just like the changes I was trying to help organizations make. The difference is that, in the 1980s, people wore the stuff they were buying. They were using it. In many of the cases I was involved in, the organization was buying the technology but not using it. It would be like buying Ray Ban glasses and deciding that you never (or rarely) wanted to wear them.

The Economist's Enigma

Ted Levitt was an economist, and like all economists, he initially thought that the important piece was the money. However, economists' work isn't the study of money. Economists' work is the understanding of people's relationships with money. It's the people that are the persistent puzzle – the economist's enigma.

In a perfect world, consumers would seek out the best value from the products they buy. They'd evaluate the utility of the offering and its cost and make a rational decision. However, economists have long since discovered that people rarely concern themselves with the rational solution. They concern themselves with the emotional solution wrapped in a rational wrapper. We need to be able to rationalize our decisions, but it's not our reason that drives the decision.

The fashionable brands from my youth reminded me of this. People would spend insane amounts of money decking themselves out with the latest and most important brands when they could have received as much benefit from clothing that was much more affordable. However, the masters of marketing had managed to sell that their brand had benefits – whether they were real, imagined, or just ephemeral.

Making Change

The brand makers had somehow managed to not only sell change in the figurative sense, but they had learned how to sell change in the quite literal sense as well. They were getting consumers to buy. However, the unpredictable nature of these brands and their value made it clear that it wasn't enough to make the change. What would ultimately matter was whether you could sustain the change. What separated the truly universal brands from those brands that came and went?

It turns out that getting sustainable change is harder than it appears. Even after heart bypass surgery, only one in ten people changed their lifestyle. Within three years, more than two-thirds of released criminals are back in jail. It's not enough to get people to try something new. It would be necessary to figure out how to get people to keep trying the change day after day. We couldn't make a New Year's resolution to a better organization only to fall off the wagon when the box of valentine chocolates appeared.

The truth is that most people who make New Year's resolutions make it about weight loss, and they've already given up well before Valentine's Day rolls around. How can you make change in your organization when you can't resist a box of chocolates?

From Personal to Professional

All change is personal, so it makes sense to start from the perspective of personal change. However, what if professional change is different? It turns out that it's not. There's the often-quoted 70% failure rate for change projects that should give anyone except professional baseball players and weathermen pause. (Professional baseball players swing and miss roughly two-thirds of the times that they're at bat.)

However, just because change is hard at both a personal and professional level doesn't mean that you can't be successful. With the right information and the right tools, you can change your odds of success.

Six Keys to Change Confidence

Pulling from three decades of experience in implementing technology and business process changes at organizations of all sizes and literally hundreds of other authors and experts, I've distilled the change management process into six keys. With these six keys, you can confidently unlock change success. The keys are:

- Creating clarity
- Project and program management
- Motivating adoption
- Communicating clearly
- Supporting stakeholders
- Organizational change

When you hold all these keys, you'll find yourself more successful at change projects. These keys unlock the doors to change and stop those doors from slamming shut before everyone has gone through.

Change Categories

Change comes in two broad categories, and these keys unlock both doors. One type of change is transactional, iterative, and optimizing. This is the type of change that is done through business process mapping, lean, kaizen, and Six Sigma. The other kind of change is transformational. These larger changes are more unsettling and more powerful in their ability to allow organizations to survive and even thrive in the future.

You may have been a part of one – or both – kinds of change and may be thinking to yourself that you sort of know how it works. You may. However, for most of us, we've fallen into the illusion of change. Like a magician's trick that makes it seem like it should be easy to link the five rings, we find that when we try it, it isn't quite as easy as it looks. This book is about revealing the magic that makes the rings trick work.

Getting Clear on the Change

Lewis Carroll and Yogi Berra had two different perspectives on defining where you want to go. Carroll, in *Alice's Adventures in Wonderland*, said, "If you don't know where you are going, any road will take you there." Yogi Berra said, "If you don't know where you're going, you might wind up someplace else." To get to change, we need to know how to guide and direct people. We need to tell them what road to travel. If we aren't clear about where we're going, it's unlikely that the people in our organization will start their journey. Even if they do, they're likely to end up someplace other than where we intend for them to be.

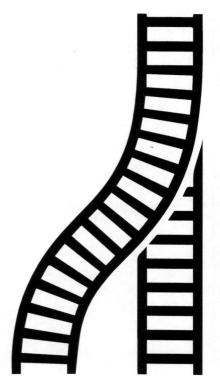

The first step to change management success is getting very clear about where we want to go. This is deceptively simple. After all, we wouldn't be asking for change if we didn't know what we want... or would we? It turns out that the devil is definitely in the details, and when it comes to change, there are a lot of details.

Hope Is Not a Plan

Every change initiative starts with hope. It starts with the opportunity to make things better by improving the situation or minimizing risk. Hope is an essential but not sufficient ingredient to any kind of change. In addition to hope, change needs a plan. It needs the series of steps that leads from the current state to the desired nirvana at the end of the rainbow.

For many, the need for a plan is a discouraging awareness. They're painfully aware that they don't know how to reach the end goal and wonder why they should bother trying. The answer is found in the successes of others, including John F. Kennedy and Walt Disney.

To the Moon I Tell 'Ya, To the Moon.

When John F. Kennedy addressed Congress with the idea of transporting a man safely to the Moon and back (by the end of the decade), no one knew how to do it.

The vision was clear, and it even had a timeline. However, the actual implementation of the vision was fuzzy at best. It wasn't possible at that moment to precisely predict the steps that would be taken to make this a reality, nor was it possible to precisely define the costs. All that could be defined was a series of next steps that moved us figuratively if not literally closer to the Moon.

This is the heart of change management: knowing the endpoint and planning just enough to develop the skills and capabilities that will allow you to reach the next set of challenges. An expert at this was Walt Disney.

From Failure to Feature-Length Movies

Few people know that the man we revere as Walt Disney was bankrupt twice and had a character stolen from him long before Mickey Mouse. Disney didn't have a straight ascension to the pinnacle of entertainment. Instead, he built an empire on the back of a mouse whom he originally called "Steamboat Willie." The genius of

---

Walt was expressed not in the amazing things that he created but in his tenacity to convert his initial dreams into reality.

Long before *Snow White and the Seven Dwarfs* became the first full-length animated movie, Walt was testing new ideas and approaches. He built new ways of generating animated artwork while the world was still very much analog. Special cameras and approaches like storyboarding were first tested on a small scale. These "shorts" would teach Disney how to be effective at telling the stories with the technologies available to him and efficient in building them.

Disney himself, a great visionary, could have never seen Walt Disney World in Florida while he was on a train to Los Angeles from Kansas City, Missouri, shortly after the bankruptcy of Laugh-O-Gram Studios. He could only ever see the next step or next few steps. He saw milestones on the journey to success, and that was enough of a plan to get by, as he adapted and adjusted with each new thing that he would learn.

Creating the Plan

When creating the change plan, there are two key areas of focus: the clarity of the vision, and the clarity of the next steps.

Vision

On the one hand, you don't know how to get to the end goal. On the other hand, you've got to paint a compelling enough picture to create the desire in everyone to get there. This can be accomplished either through fear of what's coming if things stay the same or through the belief that the future will be better than the current state if the change is successful. While the fear of what might happen if things stay the same is a powerful force, it tends to not drive action. It tends to immobilize.

A more powerful motivator to change is defining a vision that everyone desires. This is harder than it first appears. The prospect of a prosperous future for the organization is fine, but it's not the kind of compelling mission that makes everyone want to be a part of it.

Visions, as they are defined for change, first need to be compelling. That is, they need to be something that makes people want to be a part of it. Second, they must be personal. In other words, everyone in the organization must see themselves as a part of it. Only those members of the organizations who see themselves in the organization in the future will have any desire to get there.

It's one thing to use putting a man on the Moon as an inspirational vision. The mission statements of most change initiatives are generally duller and more boring than that. That is not to say that you can't develop compelling mission statements around your change. Even an initiative around changing a content management system can be compelling if it means less frustration, greater freedom, or reduced chance of error. Just because you're not putting a man on the Moon doesn't mean you can't make it compelling.

When the vision includes a transformation – as all good visions should – the natural question in the mind of the employee should be whether their department or their role personally will become redundant or will be transformed out of existence. These fears, left unaddressed, create resistance and subversion for the intended change. In the ideal case, our visions pull people towards roles and situations they desire to be in. In the minimal case, the vision must assure them that there is a desirable part of the organization they'll be able to continue to contribute in.

Next Steps

With a vision established, energy has been added to the system, but there is no focusing force to coordinate the next activities. When left with an unclear call to action, the result is almost always no action. Once excited, if a path can be illuminated, most people will follow it. This is true even if only the first few steps of the path are illuminated. Therefore, with the clear vision, there must be a path for each employee to follow that is clearly articulated and small enough to seem doable.

Providing a next step that is too large or poorly understood by employees is frustrating and demotivating. By making the changes to reach the end goal both gradual and doable, we enable and encourage employees to take those steps.

By far, the most frequent cause of failure in change initiatives is a failure to communicate. It doesn't matter how many emails, newsletters, or town halls you do if you aren't able to communicate the behavior you want in a way that people understand.

Consider a new corporate mantra – "Customer Focused" – with the nirvana of having a loyal brand and therefore the opportunity to escape the pressures of commodity pricing. This type of strategy might be employed if the organization sees a potential strength in their customer engagement but faces continuous pricing pressures. How does one become "Customer Focused"? Wall-hung pictures of cats intently looking at the camera, while cute and potentially compelling, say nothing of what to do.

If you're "Customer Focused", the accountant needs to know if they should extend longer terms to the customer or minimize terms to improve cashflow. The salesperson needs to know whether that means offering the deepest discounts available – or protecting corporate pricing. While there may be no final answer to which behaviors the customer will perceive as the organization being focused on them, there must at least be a solid starting point that describes how each person should behave that is different in the new world from the past.

Metric Measurement

The final, and perhaps most critical, aspect of creating clarity is in the development of the metrics you'll use to define success. There is a degree of clarity when you know that this is the way you're going to measure success. Metrics are typically broken down into two broad categories: leading and lagging. Through careful selection of metrics in both categories, you can prevent people from "gaming" the metrics and getting more recognition for success than they deserve. In other words, you can discourage cheating on metric values.

Making Metrics Matter

Metrics work, because the things we focus on are the things that can change. There are numerous things we do each day that we pay little or no attention to. We drive to work and don't notice the number of stoplights we stop at. We're on automatic pilot, and, as a result, we can't change or improve.

Those things we focus on through metrics can be improved upon by the very fact that we're watching them. This is something that was discovered decades ago at the Hawthorne Works, where regardless of the variable changed – or the direction in which it was changed – performance improved. The workers, knowing that their performance was being monitored, continued to improve regardless of the environmental factors in play.

The goal with developing metrics – both leading and lagging – is to create a framework that people will change in ways that are desirable both personally and for the organization.

Leading Indicators

Leading indicators are measurements of the behaviors that you believe will lead to results. If you ultimately want to increase your customer satisfaction, you look for specific behaviors you want to drive in the organization that should yield higher

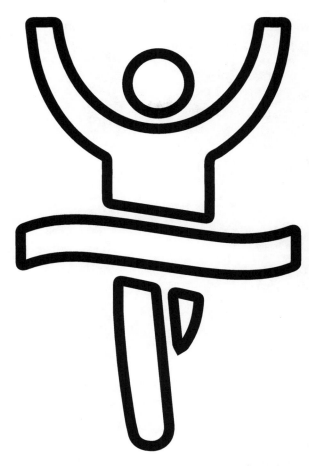

customer satisfaction. You may decide that the behavior you want to drive is follow-up after delivery of an order, so you measure the follow-up calls believing that this will result in greater customer satisfaction.

One risk of defining leading indicators is failing to recognize existing good behaviors. As a result, you may get the new, desirable behavior at the expense of another, potentially more desirable behavior. If employees are busy making follow up calls, they may stop sending customers a thank you note.

Lagging Indicators

Leading indicators don't guarantee you'll get the results you want. They only indicate that the results are likely. Lagging indicators, on the other hand, are indicators of whether you accomplished the goal. Here, the actual value targets you shoot for are often clearer. If you want to improve the customer relationship, you might target the standardized net promoter score (NPS) and look to increase the results by 2% per quarter.

Lagging indicators, by their nature, record what has been done and therefore can no longer be changed. If the leading indicators are on target and the lagging indicators aren't where you'd expect, then it may be necessary to challenge your beliefs that the behaviors associated with the leading indicators actually lead to the lagging indicators you want.

Too Many Metrics

The final consideration for metrics is how to get to a set of metrics that's manageable. It's certainly possible to try to measure every aspect of behavior inside of the organization, but it tends to be exhausting for everyone involved. It's critical

---

to find a balance of metrics that covers the behaviors and the results without overwhelming people with too many things to worry about.

Project and Program Management

Once there is clarity surrounding the intended change and the initial burst of energy has kicked off the initiative, it's time to find ways to continue to direct and harness that energy. That's the role of project and program management. While project and program management may not feel exciting, it provides a vital role of ensuring alignment and coordination as well as reducing friction.

Waterfall and Iterative

Perhaps the greatest challenge to managing a change initiative is the fact that changes are unlike most of the projects that organizations encounter. Manufacturing organizations make thousands of the same widget. They know how to get the product through the process. Hospitality companies know how to make a meal, a bed, or an experience. The projects – as small as they may be – are well defined, with all the steps known and all the expectations set. Change initiatives, by their very nature, have never been done before, and therefore the steps aren't well known – and neither are the expectations.

It turns out that the best way of managing well-known projects is a method called waterfall, and the best way for managing poorly-understood projects is an iterative, or agile, approach.

Waterfall

Waterfall project management refers to the process of continuously flowing down a path towards an eventual end. The progress may be rapid and turbulent at times, but the process and the flow are well known. A planning process happens first. During this planning process, the remainder of the steps and their durations are identified. The result is a framework against which the actual execution can be compared.

Waterfall-type projects work very well when the process is known in advance. Running the umpteenth project of the same type is often a candidate for waterfall-type management, where variations are tracked and resolved. However, the waterfall approach of project management breaks down when the steps to the end goal aren't well known. When you need to "figure things out as you go," a more effective approach is the iterative approach.

Iterative managed projects bypass the problems of waterfall-type projects and the need for complete planning. A waterfall-managed project that has a high degree of unknowns will either get stuck in the planning phase or will generate a plan that isn't accurate or reasonable but fulfills the requirements of having a plan.

Iterative

Having a solid plan is essential, yet iterative project management approaches seem to side-step this problem. They do so by planning only the pieces they can see. Cycles (or sprints) are defined in short, often two-week, periods. After each cycle, the planning process is started again, this time with the new knowledge that was learned in the previous cycle. This continuous cycling has the benefit of leveraging the new information you get in the process at the expense of both planning efficiency and rework.

Because planning is not done at the same time, the starts and stops have an associated cost. Because there are missteps due to an inability to see whether something is a dead end, there is often some rework necessary when working in an iterative approach. It's these costs that make iterative a poor approach when the project is well-known.

Inside of your change initiative, there are likely to be parts that are well known and can be managed in a waterfall approach as well as some parts that are not well known, where an iterative approach will be better. When you have different parts of the initiative that are best managed differently, it may be more appropriate to think of the initiative as a program instead of as a single project.

Projects and Programs

At first, the difference between a project and a program seems somewhat arbitrary. A program is only a collection of projects, and projects themselves can be broken into a series of phases. What does it matter whether you make your initiative one big project or several small projects inside of a larger program? As it turns out, it can matter a great deal.

Consider the situation we just described, where parts of the initiative are well-known and can be well defined. They will be most efficiently executed in the context of a waterfall approach. If there are aspects of the initiative that aren't well known, they'll need an agile approach to be efficient. Executing both approaches inside the scope of a single project is technically possible but practically impossible. Instead, breaking the projects apart allows for one management approach in one kind of project and a different approach inside another.

Another key factor that will drive you towards having a program with multiple projects instead of having a project with phases or parts is the sheer scale. If you need to have 10, 20, or more project managers and coordinators to keep all the moving parts working, you definitely want the isolation that program management offers.

Finding the dividing line between what should be a project with phases and what should be a program with projects isn't clear cut; it's a sense for what will work best in your organization based on tolerance, preference, complexity, and risk.

Tangible Tactics

A substantial element of risk as it pertains to change initiatives is converting the big picture vision into the specific set of behaviors that are needed for each person to take. This conversion process may happen up front if things are well known – or it may need to be done along the way if the type of change isn't well known, as is often the case. Either way, there's a need to deeply understand both the way the organization operates today and the way it needs to operate tomorrow. That means effective understanding of the situation accomplished through ethnographic empathy and effective communication to the rest of the organization, which means compelling content, including vivid visuals.

Empathetic Ethnography

Ethnography is most frequently associated with anthropologists and their trips to the far-off corners of the world in search of undiscovered peoples who they can study and learn more about. Their discoveries can't be read in books, not just because the books haven't been written, but because of the deep need to empathize with individuals and what their daily life is like. This is the same type of activity that organizations need to understand their people and the impacts of the changes they're being asked to make. Without this deep understanding and empathy, it's quite likely that the tactics used to encourage behavior change will backfire.

Sometimes the attempt to change behavior in a forward direction results in a reversal or a reversion into previous bad behaviors. On the surface, these behaviors seem unexplainable, but the greater the degree of understanding and empathy for the concerns of the individuals, the increased likelihood that the desired outcomes will be achieved – without any reversions to bad behaviors. Changing behavior requires knowing what motivates people and how those changes impact those motivations. Without this, there is very little that can be done to create a desire for change.

Compelling Content

The truth is that most people don't read all or even most of the information that the organization puts out. It's confusing, not applicable, or unimportant. That turns employees off to the information and the people and channels that relay it. That's why it's critical at the start to plan for creating compelling content. This comes through an awareness of human psychology and how to motivate people as well as the techniques for communication that have been honed over centuries.

Strangely, both of these approaches – through professional communicators and psychology – starts with the deep understanding and empathy that is formed through ethnographic interviews.

Vivid Visuals

They say that a picture is worth a thousand words. Whether this is true or not, diagrams are a compelling way to convey the relationship between concepts and can substantially reduce the words necessary to help people understand the intended transformation. Choices for visuals vary from the extremely detailed technical schematics and flows to the simple block diagrams that show only the major categories of interest.

Visuals allow others to get the gist of the transformation even if they don't understand all the details. The truth is they don't want the details. They wouldn't read a 100-page treatise on the initiative if you wrote it. However, they might glance at a visual, find their place in it (like a reverse game of *Where's Waldo?*), and quietly move on.

The objective for the employee is to find themselves in the new organization in a spot where they want to be. The real requirement for generating buy-in and acceptance of a change is for everyone to feel like they're a part of it.

Requirements

The requirements that are generated as a part of the process of building a project plan – or a series of project plans – is the continuation of the process of generating clarity about the kind of change that is to be brought about. Having driven to both leading and lagging metrics, there is some degree of clarity in the change that is desired; but the process of refining this message and converting the vision into tactics continues throughout the life of the project.

Clarity is created by closely examining the results that need to exist when the change is done and ensuring that the right components for these exist in the organization before the end of the change initiative. Decomposing the compounds in the molecules and the molecules into atoms allows for the organization to be rebuilt in its new image. Knowing what that new image should look like is why we generate personas.

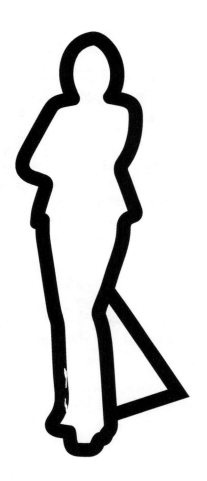

Personas

In every large-scale effort, the process of understanding every person individually is too large and complex a task to be done. Instead, we take the deep empathy and understanding that we developed, and then group the types of people we are working with into a handful of personas that we can use to focus our efforts. Personas are fictional people that are representative of a group of people. In addition to the specific characteristics of the group we're working with, they also contain what might best be considered fiction as a way of tricking our brains into thinking about them as if they were real people.

Our brains think about and communicate with individuals differently than we communicate with some abstract group. We're wired for connections with individual people, and that wiring gets gummed up when we try to speak to a group of folks who happen to occupy a role. The abstraction is more than we can handle.

As a result, we can create a fake person – Jane – and assign her a set of attributes, including a back story and other seemingly irrelevant details, to communicate more clearly with her than we might communicate with the nursing group that she represents. Our writing and thinking are clarified by considering how this one – admittedly fake – person, Jane, might respond to our messaging. This uses the same cognitive processes that we use when talking to another person and considering how they might respond to us.

Personas are the bridge between the sometimes mechanical perspective of project management and the powerful forces of the human psyche that motivate people towards, and sometimes away from, the change that we want.

Motivating Adoption and Change

By far, the most curious and intriguing topic when it comes to change is how to change individual human behaviors. It's the gristmill that organizational change relies upon, and it's the most mysterious. Most of us have spent our entire lives trying to manipulate others to do our bidding. From the first cries as a baby to the temper tantrums of a two-year-old and beyond, we've constantly tried to ply our parents and others into changing towards our desires. Despite this experience, most of us are like blind men wandering a cave trying to feel our way through the darkness.

On the other side, we've all been manipulated. We resist it to be sure, but we deep down know it to be true. We've all been like the father who bends his will when his daughter bats her eyelashes at him. We've all gotten in a car and instinctively reached for the seatbelt that we know is constraining and will wrinkle our clothes but that we feel compelled to wear. The motivation may be the law, the advertising campaigns showing what happens when we don't wear it, or peer pressure, but whatever it is, we do it. We may not like it, we may regret it, or we may grouse about it, but we do it.

The Six Keys to Confident Change Management

To be effective at any kind of change, we need to find ways of motivating other people that doesn't damage our relationship with them – too much – and still accomplishes the needed changes. We need to find ways to motivate without it crossing over to feel as if it's manipulation, even if it is.

Individual Motivators

Everyone is motivated by different things. Some people are motivated by family, some by money and power, and others by vengeance. In fact, Steven Reiss, a professor emeritus at The Ohio State University, categorized 16 basic motivators that drive people to doing what they do. His model allows for people being motivated in differing degrees by each of these factors and the unique combination of these factors lead to the motivation that they'll feel.

Of course, he's far from alone. The Meyers-Briggs Type Indicator (MBTI) categorizes people into two positions across four dimensions based on Carl Jung's work. The CliftonStrengths (owned by Gallup) categorizes people based on 34 themes and which one most identifies them. These themes are places of power and interest for the individuals and places they'll want to get back to. There are DISC profiles, Enneagrams, and dozens of other personality tests designed to help you understand how you – and others – will behave.

With so many different ways of evaluating the factors that could motivate someone, how do you choose which tools to use? Economist George Box summed it up best when he said, "All models are wrong, but some are useful." Pick the model that is the most useful to you, your team, and your organization, and don't worry about what the other models have that you like until you're ready to switch to them or add them to your existing model.

Blowing Up Barriers

If people are motivated, why don't they accomplish their behavior change goals? We all know people who are motivated to quit smoking or lose weight, yet, despite valiant efforts, they fail time and time again. The problem may be that there are barriers in their way, preventing them from accomplishing their objectives.

Small barriers, it turns out, make a big difference. If your community doesn't appreciate smoking and therefore bans smoking in public places, you'll have natural deterrents to smoking. If it's hard to purchase cigarettes, you'll have another deterrent. These deterrents can stack up to support your willpower or they can be aligned to try your willpower at every turn.

If you want to start eating healthy and you have plenty of fresh vegetable options as well as a large selection of low sodium, low fat, low carbohydrate food options, you have a greater chance of changing your diet and losing weight. When your local grocery store doesn't allow for these options, you've got a barrier to better health. While Chef Boyardee may be a kid's favorite meal, it's not the healthiest option for adults looking to lose weight. Even smaller adjustments like which foods are placed at eye level can have a profound impact on the waistline of people.

In business, most people suffer from a condition called the curse of knowledge. They literally can't unlearn what they already know about. The wheel doesn't seem like much of an invention to those who have seen and used them, but it might have been unthinkable before it first appeared in human history. This profound fact is important, because we often leave hidden barriers in the way of those whose behavior we're trying to help change. They're unaware of a simple thing that can make their change easier.

As we structure changes, we need to be on the lookout for those small barriers that are getting in the way of the change we desire and recognize that the barriers others face aren't barriers that we even recognize as barriers. The good news is that, once they have the information we have, they likely won't see them as barriers either – therefore, they're often the easiest barriers to eliminate.

Trust

One barrier that's not easy to eliminate is a lack of trust. Trust is built over a long period of time and destroyed in an instant. It's also something that has been eroding in society over the course of decades. As a society, we're losing our faith in religion, government, organizations, and even our fellow man. However, trust serves as an essential lubricant in the change process like oil is an essential lubricant for our cars. Without trust, the friction will eventually grind things to a halt.

Trust is essentially our prediction that people will behave the way we expect them to behave. This is normally a desire for them to behave in a way that is positive for us and our change initiative. Though trust is built over long periods of time, people use markers to assess three different aspects of trust. First, there is communication trust. Are you known to communicate reliably both the good and the bad news? Second is competence trust: are you competent to do what is being asked of you? Here, people start with credibility markers, like previous experience, accolades, and degrees, and gradually begin to rely on how they see you succeed or fail with other projects. Finally, contractual trust is the belief in the agreement that's being made and your willingness or ability to keep it. When these aspects of trust are aligned, people believe that you'll do what you say you are going to do or tell them when you can't. This simple realization is the foundation for trust.

One of the key roles of a change agent or leader in the success of a change project is the continued facilitation of trust and the recovery from the betrayals that people inevitably feel in an organization. Clear, consistent communications and actions pave the way for everyone to believe that you'll be successful and you'll meet your commitment to bring them along.

Governance

For most people, governance, like government, has developed a bitter aftertaste. Most of the corporate governance they've seen is the trouble you get into after you find out that you've broken the rules that you didn't even know existed. Governance has somehow lost its way and started to be about punishment and pain instead of support and guidance.

Governance derives from both Greek and Latin roots that mean "to steer" – as in the rudder of a ship. The process of getting in trouble for things you didn't know were wrong is demotivating. Getting help, support, guidance, and training can be invigorating. Great governance makes people feel like they can do more than they could have done on their own. It makes them become more willing to take calculated risks, because they believe they'll be supported in those risks as long as they're inside the guidance being provided.

If you can't focus your guidance around helping people learn how to be effective after the change, you may find that it's not possible to motivate people at all.

Learning

Adult learning is different than the kind of learning we all had in school. In school, we were prisoners for the time that we were there, and we might as well learn because we were stuck there anyway. However, as adults, rarely are we prisoners to training. Even required trainings typically have a work around (like leaving it play in the background while you're doing something else). The simple fact is that, as adults, we recognize we have a fixed capacity in time for learning. As a result, we focus our efforts in places where we have an interest, a reason, and enough background to integrate the learning into our world.

Malcolm Knowles and his colleagues said it differently. They said that adults require need to know, foundation, self-concept, readiness, orientation, and motivation. In short, adults are not generally prisoners to their need to learn as they can readily pick alternatives. As a result, we must approach the process of educating people about the change differently.

The Six Keys to Confident Change Management

Rather than imprisoning them in a 15-minute or 15-hour education session on the change, it's critical to look for opportunities to create learning solutions that fit the wants and needs of every learner. Everyone wants to understand what the new world will be like, and that means learning. However, not everyone believes that a 15-hour education session fits their schedule or is an appropriate amount of learning to match the degree of change.

Communication Strategy

Communication during a change initiative is so important that it's broken into two parts. The first part is developing a communications strategy, which will be covered here. The second part is improving the communications skills, which will be addressed in the next chapter.

Benjamin Franklin said, "If you fail to plan, you are planning to fail," yet many professionals admit that they routinely fail to plan their communications – or that the plan they do have is woefully inadequate. Dwight Eisenhower paraphrased Helmuth von Moltke when he said that "no plan survives contact with the enemy." Still, he believed that the process of planning was essential for success. If building a plan – a strategy – is so important, then why is it that so many people fail to do them?

Certainly, the awareness that the plan will be wrong is one reason for not doing a plan, but more often than not, the problem isn't a lack of awareness of the need or that the process itself creates value. It mostly comes down to a lack of understanding of what should go into a plan to make it effective. Here, we'll break down the communication strategy into the essential elements that can make it effective.

Channels

In today's world, we have a plethora of channels that we can choose for communicating with one another. From the "drive-by" conversation to electronic chat, email, digital signage, intranets, and more, the ability to communicate isn't generally the problem. The problem is what message to put in what communications channel. Marshal McLuhan said, "The medium is the message" to emphasize the importance of picking the right channel.

Yet most organizations provide no guide to which channel to use for which kinds of messages – or even bother to set expectations for responsiveness to a given channel. They are aware that different channels exist, but they treat them largely like they're a new way to transport a memo – like folding it into a paper airplane and tossing it at a coworker instead of walking it over to them or, heaven forbid, actually speaking with them face-to-face.

Channels matter. They change the way that people perceive the messages. Unfortunately, they also change the degree to which people pay attention. Our attention has become our most precious resource. Because we experience more information bombardment than our grandparents saw in their lifetime, our reticular activating system (RAS) has decided to turn down the relevancy for everything and just hope that the truly important bits aren't that problematic when they're missed.

Even the best channels and the most compelling messages that we can muster are lost in the sea of popups, notifications, and messages that we receive daily. As a result, we find that we must repeat our messages, furthering the problem of adding more noise to an already noisy world. However, repetition becomes a part of our toolbox to help punch through the attention barrier.

Repetition

Marketers have known an inconvenient truth for some time. If you want someone to hear your message, you must repeat it. No single message can make it through any one channel to everyone in your audience. However, most human resources (HR) departments lament when people complain that they never received the information after HR sent them an email. The problem is that one email isn't enough. It's never enough to reach everyone. People are too bombarded, too overwhelmed, and too incapable of recognizing the messages.

The number of times that you need to repeat a message depends on the effectiveness of the channels you're using – and you should be using more than one – the interest in the topic, the critical nature of the topic, and the copywriting prowess used to create the message. People are generally stunned at the number of times they must send a message before most (or all) of the receivers of the message have registered it.

With all of the challenges associated with getting messages through, it becomes ever more important to get clear on the messages that you send – and what you expect the receiver to do with the message when they get it.

Targeting

With repetition comes the threat of tripping a signal-to-noise switch inside the stakeholder's head and locking yourself out of further communication. The signal-to-noise ratio is the ratio between important messages – as measured from the point of view of the recipient – and the unimportant messages that they perceive as noise. A technique that is used to minimize this risk is targeting.

Targeting limits the scope of the message delivery to those who need to see it and prevents those who don't need to see it from receiving the message again. Consider two different advertising approaches: national television commercials and billboards. If you buy a national television commercial, there will be people across the country that will see the advertisement – whether the service you sell is available to them or not. Consider an attraction like Rock City, located in Chattanooga, Tennessee. It's unlikely that people from Maine or Washington state would make the trek to see your attraction from so far away. Done correctly, they'll likely not be offended for seeing the advertisement, but there certainly have been television commercials that have turned off people – sometimes to the point where they turn off their televisions.

Conversely, the strategy that Rock City employed was a billboard strategy. They paid painters to go around to the farms surrounding Chattanooga – up to several hundred miles away – and offer to paint barns for free in exchange for the ability to use one or more sides of the barn for advertising for Rock City. The benefit of this strategy is that only those who were within driving range of the attraction – and therefore likely to make the journey – saw the advertisements.

In the television scenario, much of the investment is wasted on people for whom the journey to Rock City isn't reasonable. Because of the cost, few organizations take this approach in their marketing. However, most organizations take this approach in their internal messaging. They broadcast it to everyone regardless of their level of interest. The billboard approach is a much more targeted approach that is well received, because people are more likely to be genuinely curious as to what Rock City might be about if they can reasonably visit it.

There are two basic targeting approaches that organizations can use: groups and suppression. These strategies don't work for all communications channels, but for those that are the most targeted, they are the most effective.

Groups

The most effective way of targeting is to identify groups and, instead of sending messages to everyone, only sending the message to the group of people for whom it is relevant. This is effective in mediums like email and intranets, where there can be tight control of the messaging. It's also effective when the groups are geographically based when used with digital signage.

Suppression

A different approach is to suppress messages once the behavior has been achieved. In the Rock City example, it would be the equivalent of making the advertising for Rock City disappear once people have visited – or have decided they never want to visit – the attraction. In corporate terms, there are numerous communications around topics like the annual benefits reenrollment. Most corporate citizens have gotten used to receiving a plethora of emails on the topic even after they've completed the requested work to reenroll. However, technologies exist to suppress these messages to individuals who have already completed the work.

These technologies are limited to email, intranet, and a few other channels, but they're very effective at communicating to the stakeholders that there's a real concern for minimizing the noise that people are receiving daily. Suppression techniques demonstrate that you care that the messages you're sending are received by indicating a concern for not overwhelming them with unnecessary information.

Key Messaging

Before phones stitched together multiple text messages and Twitter expanded its character count, you'd have to carefully consider how to compress your message into its most essential form. Finding this essential form – or the key message – was key because the limitations were so obvious. What has not historically been obvious is that the degree to which you can get people to receive and understand a message is equally, if not more, limited. While the ability to convey your message isn't limited to characters, the volume of the message and your ability to communicate it are similarly constrained.

In your communication strategy, it's essential to discover the key messages that you need to send so that you can be clear and on-point with every communication that you send. Key messages vary by group (persona) and by the phase of the project, so it's not a single message that you're discovering. Instead, it's the set of messages and their timings that you're looking to discover and create clarity around.

Required Communications

To the key messages, you add messages necessary for the change initiative to succeed. These messages include the preparatory messages designed to ignite interest and the messages related to training and productivity support designed to help everyone understand (and then do) the new behaviors. The key messages may overlap or interlock with these required messages to create a continuous feel in the messaging from the point of view of the stakeholders of the change initiative.

Igniting interest is the spark that gets the process rolling. From a communications strategy perspective, it often starts by letting the stakeholders develop a want for the features they're going to get. As a result, the messaging that ignites desire is often about the end solution and how it will improve the stakeholder's world. These messages sent shortly before the solution is available creates a tension and pull towards the change.

The learning and productivity aid messages are equally important as they describe the changes that are necessary to get the results. These messages are generally sent slightly ahead of launch and continue through the launch period. After the initial launch, these messages become tips to help the stakeholders leverage techniques that they may not have discovered on their own.

The final kind of required communication that should be a part of the communications plan is the success story. These communications are written from the positive feedback that is received shortly after launch and are focused on providing the social proof that the change is working. Without these success story messages, it may be difficult to convince those who are resisting the change to convert and come on board.

Building the Plan

Building the communications plan becomes an exercise in identifying the required messages and the audiences for those messages and then applying a schedule to the intersection of the messages, the targeted audiences, and the schedule. Put

The Six Keys to Confident Change Management

together in one list, it becomes possible to see which stakeholders may get over-communicated with and which stakeholders may not be receiving enough communication to feel like they're still up-to-date with the change initiative.

Ultimately, the communication plan becomes the framework for when, what, and to whom information is communicated while maintaining the knowledge that it will need to be adapted and additional communications may happen as a result of issues and events in the project that were unanticipated.

While the plan itself may not survive the realities of the implementation of the project, the planning process may prove to be invaluable.

Communication Skills

Your high school English teachers didn't do you any favors when it comes to communicating for change. Grammar and spelling may be a necessity, but they're not enough to get people to read your communications and feel like they want to be a part of a change effort. Instead, we need to look to journalism, marketing, anthropology, and psychology to find approaches that move from simple information to generating an intense desire.

Every Story is a Hero's Story

The end of a communications strategy is a communications plan that outlines what communications happen in which order to which people. However, it doesn't address the content of the messages or how the messages should be structured to help the recipients feel like they're a part of the story. For that, we lean on the work of Joseph Campbell. He studied stories from cultures around the world and found that all the hero stories followed a repeatable pattern. In summary, initially, the would-be hero denies his calling. He's challenged, meets with a mentor, confronts his own inner demons, and moves forward on his quest towards the challenge that was put before him.

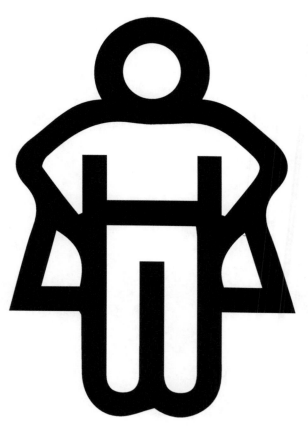

Campbell's framework identifies 12 specific steps that heroes go through on their journey. In each step, there's the inner struggle that the hero faces and the external circumstances of their struggle. The path that the hero follows may seem formulaic and prescriptive from the point of view of script writers, but it is the formula that many use – such as George Lucas for the *Star Wars* series of movies. In short, it works.

In the context of communications about change, the key to using this framework to guide the way you structure communications is to envision that the stakeholder is the hero – not the person or part of the organization initiating the change. By making sure that it's the individual contributor who is the hero in the story, you're encouraging their support of the change.

Even with a framework and some examples, it's not easy to develop a hero's story for your stakeholders. It takes work. That's why Ed Catmull of Pixar says that "Early on, all our movies suck." They suck at the start, because it's hard to write a good story. Pixar has a rock-solid process for creating good movies – and that's not something you have the time or money to invest in. The truth is that even a small step forward into this framework can be more productive than having no framework at all.

Talk Like an Egyptian

Our English teachers taught us to write with a topic sentence that starts the paragraph and a summary sentence that summarizes it, but that's just plain boring. Not only were we taught this at a paragraph level but at a paper level as well. All this repetition bores people and convinces them what we're writing just isn't worth reading. What we need is an approach that conveys the most information quickly and leaves all the details for later– if they choose to read that far. It's the technique that journalists use to target the broadest audience with the first few paragraphs and then get more nuanced and detailed as they go, and it's called inverted pyramid.

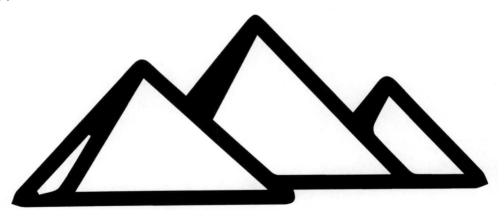

In the oversaturated, overwhelming world we live in, we don't have time to consume everything in depth. We make choices of what we read, what we skim, and what we ignore. Inverted pyramid puts the most interesting information up front so the person can make a quick decision about whether they need to read more or not.

Tantalizing Teasers

However, the top of the document isn't where most people start. They look at the subject line of an email or the title of an article to see if the topic is interesting enough to start to read the item. Here, too, our English teachers didn't do us any favors. They suggested that we should title our essays and papers with a summary of the paper. The problem is that this gets people to decide that what we're writing isn't worth reading. A different approach is to look for intrigue in your titles and subject lines, to see what happens if you don't give away the end game before you start.

To effectively communicate change, the key word isn't summary, it's intrigue. It's the kind of mystery that people can't put down, because they want to see "Who done it." That's the way you get people to click through the title of your messages and start reading.

Evoking Emotion

One of the things that your English teacher got right but was driven out of you somewhere in business communications or your first years in the organization is to write with emotion. English teachers wanted you to write great literature that tugged at your soul, and your boss wanted his report done on time. Having lost our emotion somewhere along the way, we need to find it. We need to get it back, because emotion drives us to our goals.

Jonathan Haidt has a model – the Elephant-Rider-Path model – of decision making. He explains that our rationale is a rider on top of a large, emotional elephant that is meandering down a path of defaults and expectations. The key to this model is that the rider has the illusion of control, not actual control. Anyone that has ridden a large animal – elephant or horse – knows that the animal is truly in control. The rider only gets to be in control while the animal is willing.

In business, things mostly progress along the same path with the same expectations, because neither the rider nor the elephant really care all that much. Telling the rider to change the course is fine as long as the elephant isn't worried about losing their job or what will happen next. By speaking directly to the elephant, you get the chance to address the true powerhouse of a person's psyche.

We've learned that emotions are bad in business writing, but nothing can be further from the truth. It's passion that moves us. It's just that we rationalize the decisions that our elephant makes to keep the illusion of power.

Finding the Feeling of Safe

Sometimes talking to the elephant isn't quite enough. The elephant is so preoccupied with the concerns for impending loss of job that everything else sounds like Charlie Brown's teacher – a bunch of mumbled, unintelligible words. If the elephant refuses to move with the emotion you're evoking in your writing, perhaps you need to remove the barrier that's in front of them. Perhaps you need to help them feel safe enough to walk around the mouse in their path.

Safety, as it turns out, isn't objectively measured by our brains. Instead, we consider our safety from our perspective. While some things are objectively quite safe – like airline travel – the feeling that we get is often very unsafe. Similarly, automobile accidents are a serious concern, but most of us don't worry much about an automobile accident unless we're on winding mountain roads or are driving in extreme winter conditions.

If we want to help the elephant listen to our messages – and therefore have the person make the changes we desire – we may need to change the perception of safety for their situation. Sometimes this can be done by leaning on trust, other times with guarantees, but, more often than not, simple, clear communication can help.

Most of the time, the fear that the elephant has of losing their job is because they've made up stories about what's going to happen next – because we've not told them. Samuel Clemens said, "I'm an old man, and I have known a great many troubles, but most of them never happened." If we want to ensure that people feel safe, we need to tell them how we're keeping them safe – even if it's not a complete guarantee.

If that's not enough, then we build more trust, and we look for logical anchors on which we can pin their safety, like statistics about job demand for their skills, overall economic conditions, or anything else we can use to shift their perception of their safety.

Stakeholder Management

Not everyone you'll work with during a change initiative is the same. We developed personas to account for the need to communicate with different groups in different ways at different times. However, there is more to it than the people who are directly impacted by a change. To be successful at change, we need to develop the right mix of stakeholder groups – in some cases, to bring them into existence – and we need to communicate to each group in a way that resonates with them.

More importantly, we need to revisit the motivation of each group in the context of their role within the change and address the predictable conflict, confusion, and resistance to buy-in. Stakeholder management is the major job of a change leader.

Stakeholder Salience

Before evaluating the kinds of groups that you need for a successful change, it's important to evaluate the three characteristics you're looking for in an ideal stakeholder: power, urgency, and legitimacy. When a single stakeholder or stakeholder group has all of these, they're a definitive stakeholder. While it's ideal to find these three characteristics in a single person or group, that may not always be possible. That is why we strive to find a set of stakeholders who collectively have all the necessary characteristics.

Let's look at the characteristics and why they're important.

Power

Most guides for change management will start with the need for executive sponsorship. This is really a simplification of the true need: you need someone with the power in the organization to make changes. In general, executives have this power by nature of their formal authority; however, there are often people within the organization who hold a great deal of power through their relationships and the respect others have for them but may not have an executive title.

When finding power, you're looking for those people who can use their abilities to push the change initiative when motivation doesn't work. They need to be able to carry the initiative up the small hill that it can't make by motivation alone.

Urgency

All change initiatives need a sense of urgency. By their nature, there will never be enough information or a clear picture. Someone must be willing to put a stake in the ground and say the time is now. Without this force, the change initiative will sit in the background as a good idea to get to one of these days, like cleaning out a closet, under a bed, or the garage. It's not enough to know that something must change – or even how to change it. You've got to know that the change is now.

Legitimacy

Executive support, despite its usefulness, often falls woefully short when it comes to legitimacy. The people who are doing the work are often skeptical that the executives really understand their plight. Even executives who have risen through the ranks may no longer be accepted as knowledgeable about things they once did. The argument is that things have changed so much that they're no longer "in touch" either because they are perceived to have changed or due to changes in the role itself.

Building the capacity for legitimacy on your stakeholder team is one of the key reasons why it's sometimes better to convince the "old timer" who still works the floor than it is to convince the shiny new MBA that was hired to run operations.

Teams and Roles

Change is a monumental effort that will hopefully make a monumental impact in the future of the organization. However, that level of effort cannot be done by one person or even a small group of people. It's necessary to develop a team of folks who can support the change initiative even if it's not their primary role. Here are a few of the important groups that your change will need.

Innovators

You are going to need those folks in the organization who are wired to try new things and drive the initiative forward. These people will often volunteer themselves as soon as they learn about the change, because they believe it's the right answer or they're predisposed to dislike the status quo. These innovators are quite likely to provide copious feedback. Simultaneously, they're so different from the rest of the organization that they may not be instantly followed by others in the organization.

While innovators are needed, they're insufficient. They're too different from others in the organization to be directly followed. Despite the need for proof that the change is doable and profitable, innovators are just too "out there" to be trusted immediately.

Early Adopters

Not quite as cutting edge as innovators, and therefore not as different, are the early adopters who need only a little bit of proof from the innovators that the change will be successful. The early adopters are a distinct group from the innovators who are intrigued by the ideas. Early adopters want to see the benefits but are willing to take some risks to get it. They're willing to put their neck out, but only so far.

Nurturing the early adopters and ensuring they're successful brings the early and late majorities of users and the real volume of change.

Champions

Some people need to feel like they're special. They need to feel like they're doing just a bit more than their fair share and as a result are rewarded with special access. These are the champions, who are noisier and more helpful than any other group, with the possible exception of the innovators. The language of champions isn't the "cool" as it was with the innovators. The language of champions involves legacy, impact, and compassion for others.

Developing champion groups for the initiative may not mean big expense, since the champions really only want recognition and access. However, they're a great way to gain more leverage on the staff that you have to implement the change. As force multipliers, they're important to change leaders, who often find themselves working with fewer resources than they'd like.

Conflict

Change invariably brings conflict. Someone will want to keep doing things the old way, and someone will be enamored with the new. The problem with conflict isn't that it's bad but rather that it has the potential for ruining or harming relationships. When dealing with conflict, it's important to understand that all conflict comes from just two sources: perspective or values.

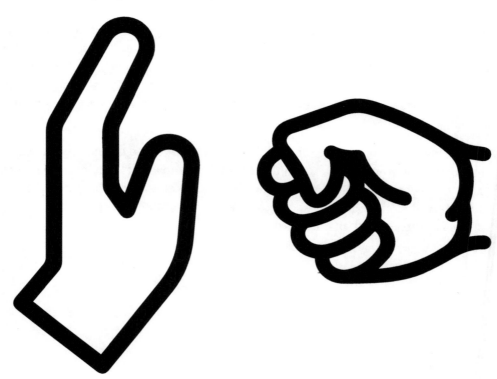

Perspective

Just because we see something in a particular way doesn't mean it actually is that way. Our belief in reality is more assembled and made up in our minds than any of us would like to admit. While we're wired to believe that our perspective is the right way to view things, it's just one way to view things.

To address conflicts based on perspective, the key is to shift the conversation from agreement with the other person to understanding. Often, our walk through conflict is blocked by our need for agreement with the other person. As a result, we can't pass through the phase of understanding to consider the usefulness or validity of the other person's point of view.

While understanding is fundamentally based on acceptance of the other person and our own fallibility, agreement is focused on our judgement of the other person and their perspective. We have little hope for shared perspective if we can't let go of judgement.

Values

Conflict based on values differences are more challenging to address, because unlike perspective, where both parties can seek to fundamentally understand, values are more entrenched in us and harder to pinpoint. While some may feel that liberty and the ability to make our own choices is paramount, others may believe that authority is more important. It's not as if either thinks that the other is unimportant, it's just the degree to which they believe their particular value is most important.

Here, too, we seek to understand while recognizing that we are unlikely to agree. Our values — using whatever measurement methods you'd like — are a part of our character, and our character is not so easily bent towards another's values.

The benefit in the values conversation is in the reality that it's the organization's values — stated or not — that are of paramount importance, not necessarily how we personally view things.

Buy-in

Even successfully navigating conflict may not necessarily generate instant buy-in for our change initiative. We may find that most stakeholders have competing priorities, and even considering whether our change initiative is the right thing might be beyond their capacity at the moment.

Our objective for the change initiative should be to identify those people who aren't bought in at any given moment, discover why, and identify what we can do about it. Everyone has their reasons for not wanting to be a part of the change. For some, it's just being too busy; but for others, it's a sense of nostalgia or a fear of losing too much of what the organization was founded upon. For still others, they have a competing agenda or differing view of the world that they're not willing to rise to the level of being a conflict. Instead, they withhold their buy-in in the hopes that the change will fail.

Whatever the reasoning, it's critical to identify and resolve the barriers that prevent people from buying into the change. Sometimes that means clarifying the difference between what they really want and what they're asking for.

Means and Ends

All stakeholders have their desires for the change initiative, but what they're asking for may not be what they really want. We have a tendency to see a path towards our eventual goal and latch on to that idea so strongly that we sometimes forget the real goal we're looking for. For instance, a teenage child may say they want a job. However, they don't really want a job – that's silly – what they want is what the job will bring them: money. In truth, they don't really want money either, because money is intangible. They want money for what it can buy them, and, in most cases, it's a car. Even the car isn't what they really want: they really want freedom, and they believe the car will give them that. These are all links in the chain between the means and the ends that they really want. The path to freedom flowed through a car, money, and a job.

When working with stakeholders, it's sometimes necessary to look beyond their request and figure out what it is that they're really asking for. If your child is looking for a job, then perhaps you can figure out what freedoms you can offer them instead.

Organizational Change

Thus far, we've spoken about the individual components that are the ingredients for a successful change initiative. Now it's time to assemble them in a way that allows you to connect the output of one to the input of another and apply these tools to your organization.

Culture

Peter Drucker said, "Culture eats strategy for breakfast." But what is culture anyway? Culture is the set of customs that are adopted in the organization and form the normal behaviors. Diving deeper, cultures are formed around the people and the processes that exist in the organization. It's an output of the processes using the people that you have.

Because culture is an output, it's not directly changeable. To change the culture, you must either change the people, the processes, or both. Most organizations are highly protective of their cultures. They look at their culture as defining who they are and how they operate – and that's true. The challenge is when aspects of the culture are getting in the way of the change the organization needs to survive.

While culture can have a big impact on the friction or organizational resistance you'll receive for your change initiative, it's generally something you'll have to learn to live with and adjust to over time. It's impractical to think that your particular change initiative is so important to the organization's survival that the organization will jettison problematic people or change the way they think about the business – unless the change is unavoidable and usually then only after it's too late.

In short, you accept the culture for what it is and work around it for each change initiative, but you should make an effort to continue to shift the culture in a positive direction with each interaction.

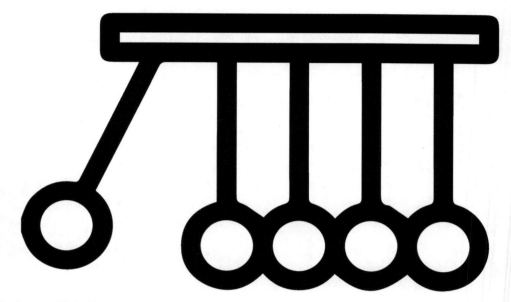

Systems Thinking

In our high school science classes (or earlier), we were taught cause and effect. We were taught how, in a Newton's cradle, one ball strikes the next, transferring its energy on down the line. This simple toy is an illustration of a single cause – the swinging ball – creating a single effect – the ball on the opposite side swinging. However, as our world gets more volatile, uncertain, complex, and ambiguous, it becomes harder to trace a single output back to a single input. Instead, we must look for feedback loops and what happens when there are multiple iterations. This is systems thinking.

Instead of the linear causality model, we look for factors and feedback loops that drive systems into and out of balance. We find ways that complexity emerges from simple patterns repeated over and over. A furnace and a thermostat form a simple system that repeats over and over again. The thermostat triggers the furnace to increase the heat until it disengages the thermostat, which disengages the furnace, until the loss of heat decreases the temperature again, and the thermostat becomes triggered. This balance of reinforcing and feedback loops reaches a homeostasis somewhere around the setpoint of the thermostat.

This is the simplest of examples. Imagine all the factors going into and coming out of your change initiative. Some of the factors won't balance out; they'll tend to accelerate the system into an uncontrolled or runaway state. For instance, the more you save, the more you make on your savings, the more you can afford to save, and therefore the more you'll make.

When considering your change, how can you set up positive reinforcing loops while reducing the kinds of factors that will limit the changes you want to create? This iterative, looping, thinking is systems thinking, and it can be a powerful way to apply the tools you've learned about.

One way to accelerate your change is to increase the degree of perceived safety, so that less time is spent protecting oneself and more resources are therefore available for productive change.

Safety

Truly effective organizational environments are based on safety and the ability to do or say what is necessary without negative repercussions. This type of environment is impossible to accomplish in the perfect sense, because individuals will bring their fears with them. You can't make an organization feel completely safe, because the people that make up the organization won't always feel safe.

Safety isn't, as we said earlier, an objective measure. Safety is a perception of how safe you are, regardless of the reality of the situation. And because it's a perception, it's subject to the same runaway rules that allow for someone to believe that a situation is very safe when it isn't or for things to spiral out of control and lack that feeling of safety.

The key for effective performance is developing a sense of psychological safety – that you can say and do the right things even if they're difficult or unpopular.

Dialogue

Another powerful tool for removing friction and increasing the effectiveness of change initiatives is the development of the conditions for dialogue. Dialogue is a special, reserved, communication state where everyone in the conversation feels safe, heard, respected, and valued. It's a place where the safety is so great that the conversation can get past the niceties and pleasantries and get to hard disagreements without those disagreements causing long-term damage to a relationship.

Dialogue is one of those things that many organizations say they aspire to or already do but one that is difficult to achieve, in part because you can't create dialogue directly. All you can do is create the right conditions for dialogue and hope that the conditions allow a dialogue to emerge.

While it's frustrating to not be able to create dialogue in the organization in a cause-and-effect-type situation, it is indicative of how change is accomplished. You can't order someone to do a new behavior and expect that it will always happen. You must create the right conditions to make the new behavior possible, including setting expectations, but ultimately, there are no guarantees that you'll see the right behaviors out of the employees of the organization.

Lifecycle

Ultimately, the change initiative itself becomes a part of the overall change of the organization and the lifecycle of all things. Each individual change initiative comes to a close at some point with its successes and failures. The key to shifting the organizational culture in a direction that makes it more conducive to future changes is how you capture the knowledge and experience of every change initiative in a way that is useful for the next change.

When changes aren't successful, they make the next change attempt noticeably more difficult. People believe in the change a little less and are willing to put forward just a little less energy towards it. So, failures are particularly important to learn from. Trying and failing at too many change initiatives can make an organization resistant to all changes.

Coda

Most people turn on a light switch and just expect light. However, when Edison started, that wasn't the expectation. Gas lights were the norm, and they had a fractured safety record. The gas produced wasn't of standard quality, and the pipes leaked. These quality issues and the inherent nature of gas lighting proved a fire safety concern as well as a suffocation risk. Turning on a gas light meant physically lighting it, and that wasn't always safe.

The creation of Edison's incandescent light bulb wasn't the application of one area of expertise. The genius of Edison's light bulb was in the simultaneous application of knowledge across multiple domains. From the work to generate electricity, create the filament, and create the vacuum around the bulb, Edison drew on the combined expertise of a team that knew about metallurgy, gas, pumps, and more.

Through this book, you've learned expertise in multiple areas as well. Each key is an area of expertise. When the keys are used simultaneously, you can light the path to successful change. A change project cannot be successful without some knowledge in each of the key areas. Just like Edison's light bulb, it doesn't work without the knowledge from every area.

Through this book, we've focused on what needs to be done. We've explained that you need to put a communications plan together; however, we didn't walk you through the process step-by-step in an exercise fashion. If you feel like you would benefit from exercises that walk you through the process of creating successful change, we'd encourage you to check out our Confident Change Management course and the 11.5 hours of video and 800 pages of information that it contains. There are 28 exercises and 84 activities that walk you step-by-step through the process of creating a plan for change in your organization that you can be confident in.

As a special thank you for reading this book, visit https://ConfidentChangeManagement.com/**SIXKEYS** receive $1,000 off the course.

It's time for you to flip your own switch and start lighting the way to confident change management in your organization.

About the Author

Robert Bogue has been delivering on technology solutions that change organizations for three decades. He's discovered the power of using the right techniques to drive the organizational change. As both a researcher and a practitioner, Robert brings the real world into the latest and best work on change adoption and motivation.

Robert has authored 27 books and has been an editor for over 100 additional books. In his corporate work, he's participated in, advised, and facilitated organizations from five-person shops to global organizations with more than 100,000 employees. A sought-after speaker, facilitator, and consultant, Robert has helped hundreds of organizations implement their changes.

Robert can be reached via email at Rob.Bogue@ThorProjects.com and via telephone at 317-844-5310.

About Confident Change Management

Confident Change Management is the collection of tools, techniques, and training that Robert has amassed in his thirty years of business. It's a complete collection of solutions that can move you from barely being aware of the need for change management to becoming a change management master.

Get more information about Confident Change Management at https://ConfidentChangeManagement.com.